Where do babies come from?

Note to parents

As soon as your child starts asking questions about babies, it's time to sit down together and read **Where do Babies Come From?** This book helps young children understand how life begins, not only for humans, but for plants and animals too. It shows how the basic processes of reproduction are repeated throughout the natural world. Answer your child's questions about the facts of life honestly but simply. Be careful not to tell children more than they want to know, or confuse them with too much detail. Your child will enjoy returning to this book again and again as his or her interest grows.

A DORLING KINDERSLEY BOOK

Project Editor Lee Simmons
Art Editor Sarah Scrutton, Peter Radcliffe
Managing Editor Jane Yorke
Art Director Linda Cole
Production Josie Alabaster

Illustrations Patrizia Donaera
Photography Steve Gorton, Susanna Price

Additional photography Jane Burton, Geoff Dann, Jo Foord, Frank Greenaway, Dave King, Andrew McRobb, Stephen Oliver, Roger Phillips, Steve Shott, Kim Taylor.

Dorling Kindersley would like to thank the following for their kind permission to reproduce their photographs: *t* top, *c* centre, *l* left, *r* right, *b* bottom, *FC* front cover, *BC* back cover.
Bruce Coleman Ltd/Kim Taylor: FCtc, bc, BCtc, 2tr,3br, 5tr, 7tl, 10tr, br, bl, cl, cr, 11tr, 12cl, 13tr, 38tcl, cl, br, 39br; Barrie Watts: FCbl, bc, tl, BCtr, 6bc, 18-19b, 19tr, 20tl, tr, bl, 21bl.
Models Jo Beal, Alex Cameron, Alicia Joseph, Hebe Wilson.

First published in Great Britain in 1996
by Dorling Kindersley Limited,
9 Henrietta Street,
London WC2E 8PS

Copyright © 1996 Dorling Kindersley Limited, London
A CIP catalogue record for this book is available from the British Library.
ISBN 0-7513-5387-6

Reproduced by Colourscan, Singapore
Printed and bound in Italy by Lego

Where do babies come from?

Angela Royston

DORLING KINDERSLEY

London • New York • Stuttgart • Moscow

Where do baby plants come from?

Where do baby birds come from?

Where do babies come from?

Where do baby animals come from?

Babies come from eggs

Most living things start life as a small egg . . .

. . . even smaller than this . . . . . . so small you cannot see it.

Where do flowers come from?

Many tiny eggs are hidden deep
inside each sunflower.

The eggs need pollen

from another

sunflower to

help them

grow into seeds.

As the bees fly from sunflower to sunflower . . .

. . . the pollen sticks   to their legs.

Flower eggs and pollen join to make seeds

The pollen from one sunflower

brushes off the bee's legs on to another sunflower.

Each egg joins with a pollen grain to make a sunflower seed.

Seeds grow into flowers

The sunflower
seed f
      a
        l
          l
           s

on to the soil

and begins

to grow.

The baby sunflower grows taller . . .

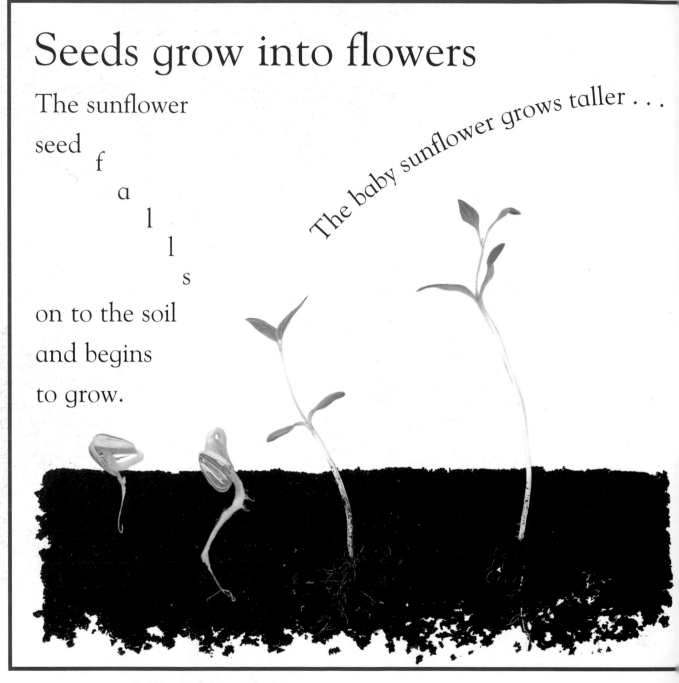

. . . and taller.

After 18 weeks,
the sunflower
is ready to make
its own seeds.

Where do ducklings come from?

It takes a mother duck and
a father duck to make a duckling.

Inside the father duck
there are tiny sperm.

Inside the mother duck there are tiny eggs.

A tiny egg joins
with a sperm inside
the mother to make
a duck's egg.

Ducklings grow inside the eggs

The mother duck
lays her eggs
in a nest.

She sits on them

Safe inside each egg . . .

to keep them warm.

. . . a duckling
is growing.

19

Ducklings grow up into ducks

After four weeks, the duckling is ready to hatch.

It pecks its way through the shell.

Ducklings grow up . . . . to become mother ducks and father ducks.

Where do kittens come from?

It takes a mother cat and a father cat to make a kitten.

Inside the father cat there are tiny sperm.

Inside the mother cat
there are tiny eggs.

Each tiny egg joins
with a sperm inside
the mother
to make
a kitten.

Kittens grow inside their mother

Several tiny kittens are growing

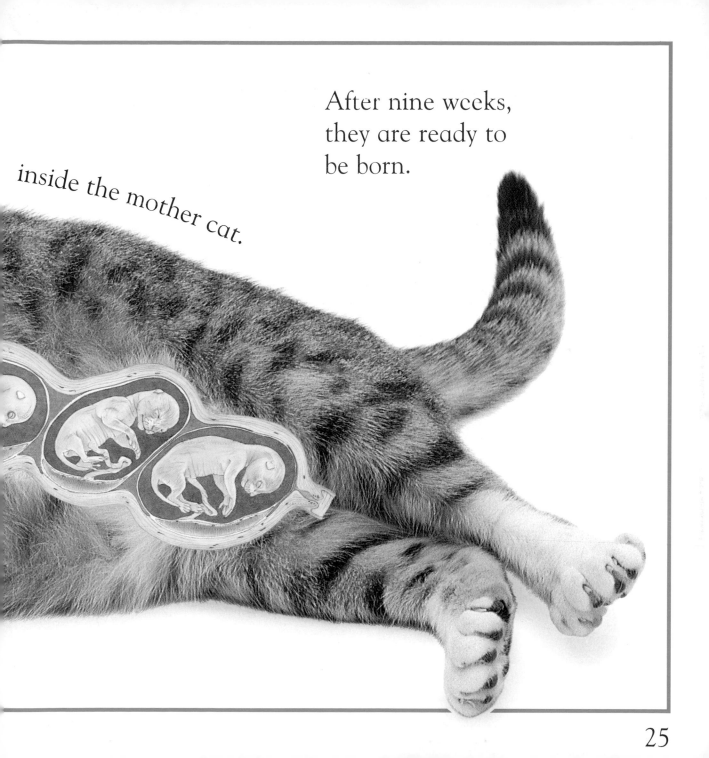

After nine weeks,
they are ready to
be born.

inside the mother cat.

25

Kittens grow up into cats

The mother licks her
newborn kittens to
clean them . . .

. . . and feeds them
with her milk.

Kittens grow up
to become
mother cats and
father cats.

Where do you come from?

It takes a mother
and a father
to make a
baby.

Inside the father
there are tiny sperm.

Inside the mother
there are tiny eggs.

A tiny egg joins with
one of the father's
sperm inside the
mother to make
a baby.

A baby grows inside its mother

The tiny baby is in a special place inside the mother called the womb.

The baby is warm and safe here. It is growing fast.

12 weeks

The mother's womb s-t-r-e-t-c-h-e-s to make room for it.

The mother can feel the baby kicking and moving.

24 weeks

The baby is ready to be born

The baby grows bigger. After nine months, it is ready to be born.

It is pushed out through a special passage between the mother's legs.

38 weeks

At last the mother can cuddle and care for her baby.

Newborn baby

33

Babies grow up into children

Babies learn to smile, sit up and play . . .

Babies grow into children, just like you.

. . . crawl, and walk.

Children grow up into adults

And children grow up · · ·

. . . to become mothers and fathers.